Discovering
the *Best* Version
of Yourself
is Only
a Step Away

Next Step
Victory

A 52-WEEK DEVOTIONAL *Journal*

ANGELA KELLY

SPEAKER | TEACHER | LIFE COACH | PASTOR

For information about this title, contact the publisher:
Angela Kelly
Email: nextstepvictory@gmail.com

ISBNs:
979-8-9901786-2-5 (softcover)

Printed in the United States of America
Cover and Interior design: 1106 Design

I want to express my deepest gratitude to my Lord and Savior for loving me unconditionally and inspiring me to hold onto hope for a brighter future.

I loved you at your darkest. (Romans 5:8)

Journaling is a powerful tool for self-discovery, allowing you to reflect on your thoughts, celebrate your growth, and uncover new insights. I'd like to dedicate this journal to my best friend Susie Williamson, who has inspired me to harness the transformative power of journaling, self-reflection, and intentional growth. May this journal guide you toward a deeper understanding of yourself, your aspirations, and the endless possibilities that await you.

Week 1

SET CLEAR GOALS

What do you need to give up to grow up and go up? Write something down you do that no longer serves life well. Incorporate something new this week that reaps lasting benefits.

Proverbs 16:1–3

My God-Size Goal this week is…

_____

Week 2

FRIENDSHIP

Take a moment to appreciate the meaningful friendships in your life. What are your strengths that nurture deep and lasting connections? Do you see any alignment between your own values and those of your closest friends? Which qualities do you deeply respect and admire?

Proverbs 17:17

My God-Size Goal this week is…

_____

Week 3

THRIVE

What three pivotal investments will you make in your body's vitality this week? Set aside moments each day and how often per week to cultivate vibrant health, then assess the shift.

1 Corinthians 6:19–20

My God-Size Goal this week is…

_____

Week 4

SOUL EYES TO REALIZE

"The two most important days in your life are the day you are born and the day you find out why."
—Mark Twain

How can you infuse your daily life with activities that ignite your passions and fuel your sense of purpose?

Romans 10:9–10

My God-Size Goal this week is…

_____

Week 5

MIND WHAT MATTERS

Uncover new possibilities by asking the right questions. What three questions can you ask today that will bring clarity and momentum to your current situation?

Philippians 4:8

My God-Size Goal this week is…

_____

Week 6

SOARING SPIRIT

What makes a day fulfilling? What do you deem crucial? What does this reflect about your character?

Romans 8:24–25

My God-Size Goal this week is…

_____

Week 7

TOP 10

Discover your guiding principles by identifying the top three values that inspire you. What are your top three non-negotiables? Explain why.

1 Corinthians 13:11–13

My God-Size Goal this week is…

Week 8

TIME SET ASIDE

20 minutes a day to...... instead of......
for the desired result to be......

Colossians 2:2–3

My God-Size Goal this week is…

_____

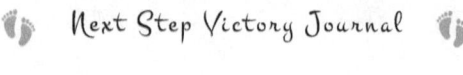

Week 9

WORDS OF PURPOSE

What inspiring words of affirmation have you spoken to others recently? What nurturing words have you spoken to your own soul? Do your words bring hope or hurt?

Ephesians 4:29

My God-Size Goal this week is…

_____

Week 10

POWER, PONDER, EVALUATE

Breaking habits that do not serve your
future self of becoming…

Who am I? I Am…Kind—Ephesians 4:32
Thankful—Hebrews 12:28
Loved—1 Thessalonians 1:4
Unique— Psalms 139:14
Curious—1 John 4:2–3
Worthy—Ephesians 4:1
Beautiful—Romans 10:15
Strong—Deuteronomy 31:6
Brave—Joshua 1:9
Amazing—Psalms 46:7–8, 10–11

My God-Size Goal this week is…

_____

Week 11

GRATITUDE IS ATTITUDE

How can you honor your journey today by acknowledging how far you've come? What valuable lessons have you gained along the way?

Ephesians 6:6–8

My God-Size Goal this week is…

_____

_____
_____
_____
_____
_____
_____
_____
_____
_____
_____
_____
_____
_____
_____
_____
_____
_____
_____
_____
_____
_____
_____
_____
_____
_____
_____
_____
_____
_____
_____

Week 12

FEAR KILLER

What obstacle stands between you and achieving your goals? What uplifting scripture can shift your mindset from fear to faith? What life ambition ignites your enthusiasm? What aspiration fuels your passions driving you forward?

Psalms 34:4

My God-Size Goal this week is…

_____

Week 13

PERSONALITY TYPE

Take a personality test online to discover more about yourself. What personal assessment did you take? What did you uncover about your personality and potential? How will this knowledge inform your path forward?

Psalms 139:13–14

My God-Size Goal this week is?

_____

Week 14

THE DIFFERENCE IS . . .

The difference between worship,
testimony, and a witness.
When honest to self and God, it's worship.
When honest to believers, it's a testimony,
and when honest to unbelievers, it's a
witness. Know your audience.

James 5:19–20

My God-Size Goal this week is…

_____

Week 15

UP THE CONVERSATION INTO INSPIRATION

Do you consider yourself a source of inspiration and motivation for others? Think of three individuals you've recently empowered with encouraging words. How did sharing positivity impact your own well-being?

Psalms 19:14

My God-Size Goal this week is…

_____

Week 16

MOMENTUM

What does it mean to truly hear and be heard? What transformative moments arise from engaged listening? How does attentive connection cultivate growth?

Hebrews 6:11–12

My God-Size Goal this week is…

_____

Week 17

GUARD YOUR EYES

What boundaries should you courageously draw?
What sacred spaces should you protect? Where
have you found balance and flexibility?

Psalms 119:123–125

My God-Size Goal this week is…

_____

Week 18

PLANTING SEEDS

"Don't judge each day by the harvest you reap,
but the seeds you plant."
—Robert Louis Stevenson

Invest in your tomorrow, today. What signs of progress and
renewal have you noticed with seeds you have planted?

1 Corinthians 2:9

My God-Size Goal this week is…

_____

Week 19

LAUGHTER IS GOOD MEDICINE

What makes you laugh? Laughter can boost the immune system, relax muscles, aid circulation, and protect against heart disease.

Psalms 126:2–3

My God-Size Goal this week is…

Week 20

EXTINGUISH ANGER

Anger is considered a secondary emotion. Primary emotion is fear, loss, or sadness. A feeling of being powerless. How can you shift that emotion realizing God is in control and you can trust Him?

2 Corinthians 2:10–11

My God-Size Goal this week is…

_____

Week 21

UNFORGIVENESS

What ways do you embody kindness and compassion in your daily life? Do you cultivate gratitude and practice swift forgiveness?

Ephesians 4:32

My God-Size Goal this week is…

_____

_____
_____
_____
_____
_____
_____
_____
_____
_____
_____
_____
_____
_____
_____
_____
_____
_____
_____
_____
_____
_____
_____
_____
_____
_____
_____
_____
_____
_____
_____
_____
_____
_____

Week 22

BOUNDARIES

Set boundaries in place, with grace and love. Know your capacity and know the capacity of others.

Proverbs 4:23

My God-Size Goal this week is…

_____

Week 23

AUTHENTICITY

You are authentic. You are unique. You shine brightly.
How can you harness your unique strengths to unlock
your full potential to shine? What are your main
three strengths? What are you doing to grow?

Jeremiah 29:11

My God-Size Goal this week is…

_____

Week 24

SCORE CARD

Write out a blessing score card. In what way have you been blessed? How have you blessed others?

1 Corinthians 13:7

My God-Size Goal this week is…

_____

Week 25

CHANGE WITH THE SEASON, OR THE SEASON WILL CHANGE YOU

What season of growth are you in? What trials and triumphs shaped you in the last season? What did you let go? What clarity have you discovered in this new season?

Ephesians 4:15–16

My God-Size Goal this week is…

_____

Week 26

"KICKS OR LIFTS"
By Betty White

Are setbacks a chance to leap forward, obstacles a test of resilience, and sidesteps a path to innovation? How will you reframe your day? Dilemma, distraction, drama, discernment, or direction?

James 4:7–16

My God-Size Goal this week is…

_____

Week 27

DRIVE, HEAL, AND INSPIRE

As you travel, how do you mentally prepare to arrive at your next destination feeling energized? What positive self-talk guides you from point A to point B? What growth-oriented thoughts emerge during your journey?

Proverbs 14:29–30

My God-Size Goal this week is…

_____

Week 28

BUILD A BRIDGE

How do you define fulfillment? What activities or experiences make you feel truly alive and content? How can you incorporate others in your journey?

Colossians 3:15

My God Size Goal this week is…

_____

Week 29

COMFORT

What gives you comfort? What activities allow you to fully unwind? What intentional choices can you make this week to prioritize your comfort and calm?

James 1:17–18

My God-Size Goal this week is…

_____

Week 30

LEVERAGE OTHERS

Maximize your time, minimize your distraction.
When is your optimum time of input and output?
What are you reading? What are you writing and
how do you influence leveraging others?

Ecclesiastes 3:12–13

My God-Size Goal this week is…

_____

Week 31

MINDFUL MEDITATION

What is truth? What is truth in action? What does that look like to respond in truth? How can we cultivate a culture of truth?

Hebrews 12:1–2

My God-Size Goal this week is…

_____

Week 32

BRIGHTER AND BETTER

Take a moment to acknowledge your concerns and worries by writing them down and placing them in a jar. Seal it, pray, and walk away. How did it feel to release?

Romans 15:13

My God-Size Goal this week is…

_____

Week 33

MAKE A MOVE

In what area do you feel stuck? What clarifying question needs to be asked to gain understanding? What bold action can you take this week to gain momentum and bring your vision closer?

1 Peter 4:10

My God-Size Goal this week is…

_____

Week 34

PERSPECTIVE

Most of your unhappiness in life is that you're listening
to yourself instead of talking to yourself.
—Martin Lloyd Jones

How do you nurture a positive mindset through
self-talk? Do you acknowledge when negative
thoughts are rooted in childhood experiences?

Psalms 19:14

My God-Size Goal this week is…

_____

Week 35

COMFORT ZONE

How have you become comfortable?
In what areas do you see this as a bonus?
What areas do you see this as a concern?

Proverbs 15:13–16

My God-Size Goal this week is…

_____

Week 36

CORE VALUES

Write down your core values. Reflect on your guiding principles. What values shaped your journey five or ten years ago? Which three core values now ignite your passion and purpose, and what makes them so vital to your growth?

2 Timothy 2:22

My God-Size Goal this week is…

_____

Week 37

LETTING GO!

Where do you feel challenged in life, and what areas would you love to reclaim control over? What small steps can you take today to move forward?

2 Corinthians 1:12

My God-Size Goal this week is…

_____

Week 38

MOTHERS

Fun fact: Mother's breast milk hormone released in a.m. differs in the p.m. milk. God is in the details. What area have you discovered God in the details?

Jeremiah 1:5

My God-Size Goal this week is…

_____

Week 39

LIFE ISN'T FAIR

How do you define each situation? Are you driven by fairness or remarkable outcomes? Where does fairness end and exceptional goodness begin?

1 Timothy 4:4–5

My God-Size Goal this week is…

_____

Week 40

RAINBOWS AND RAIN

Before the rainbow's display, rain rejuvenates the earth. What personal storms are you navigating? What life-changing blessings and opportunities await?

Genesis 9:15

My God-Size Goal this week is…

_____

Week 41

COMMUNICATION

What platform do you use to communicate well?
Facebook, text, email, FaceTime, phone call?
What is the best platform to use and why?

Deuteronomy 4:12–14

My God-Size Goal this week is…

_____

Week 42

BREAKTHROUGH

What area of breakthrough are you needing most?
How can you pray more effectively to
prepare for this breakthrough?

Proverbs 4:26–27

My God-Size Goal this week is…

_____

Week 43

CONTROL PART 2

The buffalo run into the eye of the tornado. Look it up, read about it. How does that speak to you? What can we learn from the instincts of the buffalo?

Proverbs 25:21–22

My God-Size Goal this week is…

_____

Week 44

SISTERING

Are you the one reinforcing others right now, or is your heart heavy and spirit in need of refreshing? Think of a time that others reinforced you. How did you feel?

Deuteronomy 29:2–6

My God-Size Goal this week is…

_____

Week 45

CULTIVATING HABITS

In what way can you improve your healthy living habits? Think of one area you would like to implement. Make a list of all the potential benefits. What are you most excited about with this decision?

Matthew 6:25–27

My God-Size Goal this week is…

_____

Week 46

THREE-MINUTE RULE

What are you doing for three minutes daily to improve your overall well being? Write it down. Commit to do these improvements with someone else as well.

Romans 16:19–20

My God-Size Goal this week is…

_____

Week 47

DIFFICULTY IN DIRECTION

What is difficult? What is your direction?
What benefits are on the other side of difficult?
What direction are you headed?

Ephesians 1:22–23

My God size Gail this week is…

_____

Week 48

PRAISE VS. CONFRONTATION

What is a praise song you can play today to lift up your mood? What are three things you can say today to praise and uplift others?

Ephesians 4:23–25

My God-Size Goal this week is…

_____

Week 49

RUN FROM OR TO?

Fully realize your God size dream. Jesus didn't call the qualified. He qualified the called.

Ephesians 2:1–5

My God-Size Goal this week is…

_____

_____

_____

_____

_____

_____

_____

_____

_____

_____

_____

_____

_____

_____

_____

_____

_____

_____

_____

_____

_____

_____

_____

_____

_____

_____

_____

_____

_____

_____

_____

_____

_____

_____

Week 50

MARRIAGE: THE 1-1-1 RULE

Sit and talk in meaningful conversation once a day with your spouse. Go out once a week. Vacation overnight once a year. What benefits are you experiencing?

Ephesians 5:15–17

My God-Size Goal this week is…

_____

Week 51

CHILD REARING

Are you seeing growth in your parenting?
What is the goal? How do you feel?
How are they a blessing to others?

Genesis 1:27–28

My God-Size Goal this week is…

_____

Week 52

YOU DID IT!

List the top three areas you have grown this past year.
What did you give up? How did you grow up?
And how did you get unstuck?
What's the number one achievement out of the three
areas of growth you are most excited about?

Joshua 1:9

What was the number one God-Size Goal
you saw fulfilled this year?

_____

www.ingramcontent.com/pod-product-compliance
Lightning Source LLC
Chambersburg PA
CBHW020415150626
46554CB00014B/1239